D1105789

Let's Fondue!

Let's Fondue!

Susan Lukens

photographs by

Jerry Stebbins

NODIN PRESS

3 3210 1487368

Let's Fondue! © Nodin Press, 2004

All rights reserved. No part of this book may be reproduced in any form without the written permission of Nodin Press, except for review purposes.
Portions of this book were originally published as "Fondue on the Menu" by Beverly Kees and Donnie Flora.

Nodin Press is a division of Micawber's, Inc.
530 N. Third Street, Suite 120
Minneapolis, MN 55401

Author's acknowledgements

Publishing Director: Norton Stillman
Editor: John Toren
Food Stylist: Susan Lukens
Prop Stylist: Susan Lukens
Photographer: Jerry Stebbins
Layout: John Toren

.

I would like to thank the following people for their assistance in making this book a reality: Norton Stillman, for the idea; John Toren, for his creative editing expertise; and Jerry Stebbins, for his photographic skills and for his confidence in me. Also many thanks to my family and friends in the tasting of all the recipes.

ISBN- 1-932472-30-4
UPC # 887077000160

This book is dedicated to my husband Greg
and to my son Blaine.

Contents

INTRODUCTION

First a simple question. Why Fondue? Because fondue has attributes shared by few other means of food preparation. It's exotic, versatile, and easy, it takes place right before your eyes—and everyone gets to join in the fun. Today's fondues are healthier than ever, often utilizing fresh vegetables and flavorful broths in place of oil.

Legend has it that fondue was invented by a Swiss shepherd who had grown weary of his monotonous winter fare of hard bread, cheese and wine. One day he lit a fire under his iron pot, tossed in the cheese, added some wine and dipped the bread into the bubbling mixture. What a wonderful accident! The idea soon spread, and it was eventually adopted by hospitable innkeepers throughout Switzerland.

The word "fondue" derives from the French verb *fondre*—to melt. The first Swiss fondue from the Neuchâtel region was a blend of Emmentaler and Gruyère cheese melted in white wine and kirsch. Other methods were later developed that are not true fondues because nothing is melted. Fondue bourguignonne makes use of hot oil, and broth "fondue" (an adaptation of Mongolian hotpot) is well suited for dipping both vegetables and meat.

In fact, any favorite soup can be transformed into a fondue broth by adding herbs, wine, or flavor-enhancers and simmering the ingredients for a few minutes to infuse the flavors. Serving vegetables (rather than bread) swished in such flavorful broths (rather than oil) can provide a healthy twist to the classic method.

Wine, though not essential, is an important component to many fondue menus, both to accompany the meal and also to be used in the broth. Use your personal preference as your guide.

In this book I have compiled a selection of my favorites, both classic and nouveau. I've also included a variety of salads, which are designed to be served as a refreshing palate-cleanser at the end of a meal, and a few delectable chocolate and fruit fondues to satisfy even the most demanding sweet tooth.

Fondue is designed to be shared with a group of your favorite people, and it can easily become a tradition. Select a special occasion—New Year's Eve, a spouse's birthday, Christmas Eve, or a traditional family gathering—and celebrate this event each year by enjoying fondue. The slow pace and participatory nature of the experience make it uniquely appropriate for such times.

GUIDELINES

Whichever fonduing method you select, here are a few guidelines for insuring a successful event:

• Fondues, oils, and stocks should be prepared at the stove and then transferred to the table-top burner. Use extreme caution when doing this!

• Heat the serving pot before adding the fondue from the stove so the temperature doesn't drop.

• Oil must fill no more than one-half of the pot, and stock no more than two-thirds.

• Light the table-top burner before the hot-dish arrives, and set it on the table on a heatproof mat.

• Chocolate and cheese fondues must be kept on low heat at all times, so they do not burn or curdle.

• A contemporary fondue party often starts with a cheese fondue followed by either a broth or oil fondue. To round out the meal, serve steamed vegetables, potatoes, rice, or ravioli...and of course, a variety of sauces for dipping. Salad is served at this point, and then a dessert fondue.

• Four to six people is the limit for one pot, in order to prevent crowding of meats and vegetables, which would lower the temperature of the oil.

Cheese Fondues

• When making a cheese fondue, it's best to use a heat-proof earthenware or enameled cast-iron pot, as they will heat at a slow rate and prevent burning.

• Cheeses that melt well for fondue are summarized in the cheese chart on page 18-19. Use this reference to familiarize yourself with different cheeses or to find substitutions. The original Swiss fondue is made from Emmentaler and Gruyère cheeses. (See recipe, page 20)

• Melt the cheese at a low temperature for a short time. When the wine-cheese mixture starts to bubble around the edges of the pot, simmer for one to two minutes. Do not allow to boil.

• Some tips for a successful cheese fondue are:

  • If the cheese separates during preparation, warm over medium heat, whisking constantly.

  • If the fondue is too thick, whisk in a little wine.

  • If it's too thin, add a little more cheese or 1 teaspoon cornstarch blended with 1 tablespoon water.

  • If the fondue becomes stringy, turn heat to low and whisk until the cheese is creamy.

- If the cheese becomes lumpy, increase the heat slightly and whisk constantly.

- If it curdles, add 1 teaspoon lemon juice and whisk it until smooth.

- Bread cubes for dipping should be calculated at 6-8 ounces of bread per person. Blanched vegetables or tart apples are a delightful dipping alternative.

- The fondue will stay creamy if guests stir the fondue in a figure-eight pattern with their fondue forks when dipping a cube of bread.

- Salads should be offered as a refreshing final course.

Chicken, Beef, Fish, and Vegetable Fondues

Oil Fondues

- Your best and most versatile investment is a copper, stainless steel or enamelled cast-iron pot. These are the only materials that will withstand the heat required to cook oil fondues. An electric fondue pot is the most convenient for oil and broth fondues because temperature can be easily controlled with a thermostat. Please, though—don't ever try cooking an oil fondue in an earthenware pot. The pot may crack under the high heat and the results could be disastrous. Earthenware was never intended to withstand the high temperature needed for oil fondues.

• Peanut oil is recommended but vegetable oil is acceptable, or add a little flavored oil to the basic cooking oil.

• To test if temperature of 375° F has been attained, drop a bread cube into the oil. It should turn golden within 30 seconds.

• Prepare a paper-towel lined dish for guests to pat off excess oil.

Broth Fondues

• When making a chicken, beef, or vegetable broth, homemade is definitely most flavorful and economical. For convenience, canned broth can be substituted.

• Keep the broth simmering (not boiling) during fonduing.

• When making an oil fondue use an enameled cast-iron, stainless steel, or electric fondue pot, capable of withstanding the required 375° F temperature.

• For chicken, beef, or fish fondues, calculate 4 to 6 ounces per person, provided you are serving an appetizer cheese fondue and other side dishes.

• Select tender cuts of meat, such as tenderloin, that cook quickly. Choose firm fish such as tuna, halibut, or swordfish that will not fall apart during cooking.

• Meat should be brought to room temperature before fonduing, and if marinated, should be patted dry with paper towels before cooking.

• Thoroughly dry meat and fish before cooking in hot oil to minimize splattering.

• Provide at least three complimentary sauces and dips to enhance the experience.

• Reheat the oil or broth on the stove if the temperature drops noticeably.

• Cook meats 1-2 minutes in oil fondues and 3-5 minutes in broth fondues. Chicken and fish require 1-2 minutes in oil and 2-4 minutes in broth.

Dessert Fondues

• When making a chocolate fondue, a metal pot is not a good choice because chocolate scorches easily. The best dessert set is a small ceramic or stoneware pot placed over a votive candle which will provide sufficient heat to warm the chocolate gently at the table. If chocolate burns it cannot be rescued.

• Use the finest chocolate you can find, and prepare the fondue immediately before serving. A double boiler works the best for warming cream and melting chocolate.

• If the chocolate is too thin, allow it to simmer for a few minutes. If it's too thick, stir in a little cream.

• Get creative when it comes to the liqueur in dessert fondues. There are many options available, so feel free to substitute. Choices include Amaretto, Kahlua, Grand Marnier, cognac, crème de cacao, Cointreau, coconut rum, kirsch, and Godiva.

• Fruit is the healthiest and best compliment to chocolate and dessert fondues. Experiment with fruits such as orange or tangerine sections, grapes, strawberries, blueberries, kiwi, bananas, cherries, peaches, tart apples, pineapple chunks, pears, star-fruit, mango, and honeydew. Other delectable dippers include shortbread cookies, angel food cake, biscotti cookies, toasted pound cake, ladyfingers, sponge cake, banana bread, nuts, dried apricots, and chocolate chip cookies.

• The chocolate will adhere to the fruit more readily if you chill fruit dippers before serving.

CHEESE CHART

This chart is designed to assist you in familiarizing yourself with a variety of cheeses that melt well. It should also be helpful when searching for substitutes.

Bel Paese

A popular Italian table cheese. Soft, mild and sweet. It is a good melting cheese and can be substituted for Mozzarella.

Brick

An American cheese. Mild and firm when young; acquires an earthy flavor as it ages. Softer than cheddar, firmer than Limburger; has small holes. Great melted in fondues.

Cheddar

A white English cheese. Nutty, tangy, and rich when well-aged. The orange American version is also good.

Emmentaler

Also known as Swiss cheese. Named for the Emmental Valley in Switzerland. Flavor is something like that of walnuts or hazelnuts. Holes vary greatly in size.

Fontina

Italian sweet, delicate cheese. Made from whole cow's or ewe's milk. Also comes in semi-hard variety, which has a nutty flavor. Substitute Gruyère.

Gorgonzola

Italian soft and creamy cheese; white shot with blue. Spicy piquant flavor.

Gruyère

French or Swiss hard cow's milk cheese; has small holes. An excellent fondue cheese.

Manchego

A Spanish sheep's -milk cheese; a fine melting cheese.

Monterey Jack

American Cheddar-type cheese made from whole or partially skimmed milk. No coloring added.

Muenster

French semi-hard, fermented cheese with bright red rind.

Parmesan

Italian cheese. Hardest of all cheeses when properly cured. For best flavor purchase in blocks and grate as needed. Argentinean versions are good. American Parmesan is less flavorful.

Pepper Jack

Domestic natural cheese, seasoned with green and red chili peppers. Note: Pepper Jack cheeses from Wisconsin Farms is 100% quality cheese. Look for it in your grocer's cheese section.

Ricotta

Italian rich, creamy, fresh cheese. Usually made from cow's milk.

Romano

Italian hard cheese, for grating. Pecorino, made from ewe's milk, is best.

Roquefort

French blue-veined, creamy cheese made wholly from ewe's milk. Well-aged, with a sharp distinctive flavor.

Swiss

Domestic Swiss cheese, though not as flavorful as Emmentaler, is nevertheless a fine fondue cheese.

Tilsit

German medium-firm cheese with small holes. Somewhat like Brick. Light yellow with mild to medium-sharp taste. Great for fondue.

classic swiss fondue

Rub the cut side of the garlic around the inside of the fondue pot; discard garlic.

Heat the wine and lemon juice in the pot on the stove until boiling. Reduce heat to medium-low.

Put the grated cheese into a bowl, add the flour, and toss well.

Add the cheese mixture gradually, by handfuls, to the simmering wine, making sure each addition has melted before adding more. Stir constantly with a whisk in a figure-eight motion.

When all the cheese has been added and the mixture is smooth and creamy, stir in the kirsch. Add nutmeg and pepper.

Transfer the pot to its table-top burner.

1 clove garlic, halved
1 cup dry white wine
1 tsp lemon juice
8 oz Gruyère cheese, coarsely grated
8 oz Emmentaler cheese, coarsely grated
1 Tbsp flour
2 Tbsp kirsch
¼ tsp freshly grated nutmeg
dash white pepper

Serve with

Cubes of sourdough French bread, vegetables, Granny Smith apples, red grapes, and pear slices for dipping

Greek salad (page 65)

Serves 4 to 6

CHEESE
FONDUES

gorgonzola-tilsit fondue

Grate cheese coarsely and dredge with flour.

Heat wine and garlic until almost boiling.

Add cheese by handfuls, making sure each addition has melted and blended before adding more.

When all the cheese has been added and the mixture is smooth and thick, stir in the kirsch; add nutmeg, salt and pepper.

½ lb Gorgonzola cheese
½ lb Tilsit cheese
½ lb Gruyère cheese
2 Tbsp flour
1½ cups dry white wine
1 clove garlic, minced
2 Tbsp kirsch
Salt, pepper and nutmeg to taste

Serve with

Pear wedges, apples, chunks of French bread for dipping

Orange and Blueberry Salad (page 71)

Serves 6

Heat the beer in the fondue pot until almost boiling.

Dredge cheese in flour; add cheese gradually, by handfuls, stirring after each addition until it is completely melted.

The fondue is quite hot and would serve well as an appetizer.

Note: Pepper Jack cheese from Wisconsin Cheese Group is quality cheese. Look for it in your grocer's cheese section.

1 cup lager beer
1 lb hot pepper cheese, such as Wisconsin Cheese Group, grated
1 Tbsp flour or cornstarch

Serve with

Tortilla chips, broccoli, red pepper strips, celery sticks, and bread cubes for dipping

Mixed Green Salad (page 67)

Serves 4 to 6

swiss with spinach fondue

Rub the inside of the fondue pot with garlic pieces; discard garlic.

Add the wine and heat until almost boiling. Reduce to simmering.

Dredge cheese in flour; add by handfuls to the wine, blending each addition well before adding more.

When all the cheese is blended, stir in kirsch and well-drained spinach. Crush the rosemary and stir it in.

Taste for seasoning and add salt if desired.

1 clove garlic, slivered

1 cup dry white wine

1 lb Gruyère or Emmentaler cheese, coarsely grated

1 Tbsp flour or cornstarch

2 Tbsp kirsch

½ of 10-ounce package frozen spinach, thawed, drained and squeezed dry in paper towels

1 tsp rosemary, crushed

Serve with

Mushrooms, yellow bell peppers and apple wedges for dipping

Bread sticks

Mixed Green Salad (page 67)

Serves 4 to 6

cheddar-beer fondue with chives

Rub inside of the fondue pot with garlic; discard garlic.

Heat the beer in the pot until almost boiling. Add the cheese, dredged in flour, by handfuls, making sure each addition has melted and blended before adding more.

When all the cheese has been added and the mixture is smooth and thick, stir in the Worcestershire sauce; add dry mustard.

Garnish with chives.

1 clove garlic
1 cup lager beer
1 lb well-aged sharp Cheddar cheese, coarsely grated
1 Tbsp flour
1 tsp Worcestershire sauce
½ tsp dry mustard
2 Tbsp chopped chives

Serve with

Chunks of wholewheat bread, celery and carrot sticks, radish and apple wedges for dipping

Cucumber Salad (page 69)

Serves 4 to 6

smoked gouda fondue

Combine smoked Gouda, Gruyère, and flour in a bowl. Toss well to coat cheese with flour.

Rub the inside of a large saucepan with cut sides of garlic. Discard garlic.

Add wine and lemon juice. Bring to a simmer over medium heat. Reduce heat to medium-low.

Add cheese mixture by handfuls to saucepan, stirring constantly until cheese is melted. Transfer to fondue pot and serve immediately.

6 ounces imported smoked Gouda cheese, grated
8 ounces Gruyère cheese, grated
1 Tbsp flour
2 cloves garlic, halved
¾ cup dry white wine
1 tsp lemon juice

Serve with

Wedges of apple, mushroom, steamed zucchini, red peppers, and 2 lbs crusty sourdough bread, cut into cubes for dipping

Asian Sesame Salad (page 73)

Serves 4

sweet and sour chicken fondue

Cut the chicken breast into cubes and place in a ziplock bag.

Mix together the garlic, sugar, soy sauce, vinegar, and wine, and pour over the chicken. Refrigerate for at least 30 minutes, rotating the bag a few times while marinating.

Mix the eggs and the water together until light and frothy, then sift in the flour and cornstarch. There will be a few lumps. Place in small bowls.

Drain the meat and place in small bowls.

Heat the oil to 375° F in the fondue pot, then carefully place on the lit burner. Spear a piece of chicken onto a fondue fork, dip in the batter, then fry in the oil until crisp and golden.

Serve with dipping sauce, rice, and salad.

1½ lbs chicken breast, cubed
4 garlic cloves, peeled and crushed
1 Tbsp brown sugar
2 Tbsp soy sauce
2 Tbsp white wine vinegar
1 cup white wine

For the Batter

2 medium eggs, beaten
1 cup ice-cold water
1 cup all-purpose flour
½ cup cornstarch
3-4 cups oil, for frying

Serve with

Sweet & Sour Sauce (page 58)

Fresh-cooked rice

Chinese Salad (page 66)

Serves 6

CHICKEN
FONDUES

thai chicken hotpot

To make marinade, combine lemon zest, lemon pepper, garlic, salt, and pepper in a small bowl; mix well.

Put marinade in a ziplock bag, add chicken and make sure that all pieces are well-coated. Refrigerate for 1-2 hours.

Peel lemongrass, leaving only lower 3 inches. Cut off 1 inch from bottom and chop remaining white part.

In a large saucepan, combine chicken broth, lemongrass, shallots, garlic, mint, fish sauce, sugar, and red pepper flakes, and bring to a boil. Simmer, covered, for 20 minutes. Transfer to a fondue pot, light flame and keep broth simmering.

Meanwhile, cook the noodles in boiling water for 3 minutes; drain and set aside.

Serve with a platter of bok choy, red pepper, bean sprouts, and mushrooms. Fondue chicken and vegetable pieces individually, and dip in sauces, until half of the chicken remains. Then add chicken and remaining vegetables to the pot. Simmer 5 minutes. Add 1 cup pre-cooked noodles. Serve as a noodle soup to end the meal.

2 tsp lemon zest
1 Tbsp lemon pepper
2 cloves garlic, pressed
salt and freshly ground pepper to taste
1 lb boneless skinless chicken breasts, thinly
    sliced into 1 inch pieces

Broth
5 cups chicken broth
2 stalks lemongrass
2 shallots, minced
1 clove garlic, minced
2 tablespoons chopped mint leaves
1 tsp bottled fish sauce
½ tsp sugar
⅛ tsp red pepper flakes

1 cup dried thread egg noodles, pre-cooked
½ cup each: bok choy, red peppers, bean sprouts,
    porcini mushrooms

Serve with

Thai Peanut Sauce (page 59), Sweet & Sour Sauce (page 58), Curried Cream Sauce (page 63)

Rice

Asian Sesame Salad (page 73)

Serves 4

Cut the chicken into strips and place in a ziplock bag, along with the chilies, garlic, Tabasco sauce, cilantro, honey, lime juice, and 6 tablespoons of the oil. Mix well and marinate in the refrigerator for 30-60 minutes.

Drain the chicken and arrange in small bowls. Garnish with cilantro sprigs.

Heat the oil to 375° F in the fondue pot and carefully place the pot on the lit burner. Thread the chicken strips onto the fondue forks or skewers and cook in the hot oil for 2 to 4 minutes.

Simply dip in various dipping sauces or roll up in a grilled tortilla with lettuce, scallions, and the sauce of your choice.

2 lbs boneless, skinless chicken breasts, cut into strips (easiest when partially frozen)
2 chilies, finely chopped
4 garlic cloves, peeled and chopped
3 tsp Tabasco sauce
3 Tbsp chopped fresh cilantro
2 tsp honey
3 Tbsp lime juice
6 Tbsp oil
3-4 cups oil for fondue

Serve with

Tomato or Mango Salsa (page 53), Aïoli Sauce (page 57), El Diablo Sauce (page 54), and Gucamole del Diablo Sauce (page 56) for dipping

Warmed or grilled small-size tortillas, shredded lettuce, shredded scallions

Orange & Blueberry Salad (page 63)

Serves 6

indian chicken mango soup

Heat oil over medium heat in a large saucepan. Add shallots and saute for 2 minutes. Add chicken broth, ginger, curry powder, turmeric, cayenne, and cumin. Simmer, covered, for 20 minutes to allow flavors to blend. Add mango to broth and simmer, uncovered, for another 5 minutes.

Transfer broth to fondue pot, light flame and keep broth at a simmer.

Meanwhile, cook the noodles in boiling water for 3 minutes; drain and set aside.

Spear chicken with fondue fork and fondue until cooked through (2 to 4 minutes).

Serve with an array of vegetables on a platter. Fondue chicken and vegetables to desired doneness, and dip in sauces. When about half of the chicken remains, add it to fondue pot with remaining vegetables. Simmer for several minutes, then add 1 cup pre-cooked dried thread egg noodles. Serve as a noodle soup to finish the meal.

1 Tbsp vegetable oil

2 shallots, minced

5 cups chicken broth

1 Tbsp finely minced ginger root

¾ tsp curry powder

½ tsp ground turmeric

¼ tsp cayenne pepper

¼ tsp ground cumin

¾ cup sliced mango (one mango)

1 lb boneless skinless chicken, cut into strips
     (easiest when partially frozen)

1 cup dried thread egg noodles, pre-cooked

½ cup each: red peppers, bok choy, mushrooms, and carrots, cut into strips

Serve with

Thai Peanut Sauce (page 59), Curried Cream Sauce (page 63), Mango Salsa (page 53) and Aïoli Sauce (page 57)

Mushroom Salad (page 68)

Serves 6

BEEF
FONDUES

fondue bourguignonne

Cut the steak into cubes. Arrange on a platter with garnish.

Fill a metal fondue pot no more than half full with oil. Put the garlic clove and bay leaf into the oil. Heat the oil to 375° F, then carefully transfer to the tabletop burner.

Spear the meat onto fondue forks and cook in the oil for 1 to 4 minutes. Serve with a selection of sauces, cornichons, olives, and bread.

2 lbs sirloin steak or beef tenderloin, cut into 1 inch cubes
3-4 cups peanut or safflower oil, for fondue
1 clove garlic, peeled
1 bay leaf

Garnish with

1 bunch flat-leaf Italian parsley
2 roma tomatoes, cut into wedges

Serve with

Wasabi Mayonnaise (page 63), Sweet and Sour Sauce (page 58), Curried Cream Sauce (page 63), Thai Peanut Sauce (page 59)

Cornichons, olives, and bread

Mushroom Salad (page 68)

Serves 6 to 8

korean bulgoki

In a bowl, combine soy sauce, water, onions, garlic, sugar, ginger, and pepper; stir well and put in ziplock bag.

Place steak in bag and toss well to coat. Refrigerate 2 hours or overnight.

Remove beef from marinade, and pat with paper towel to remove excess marinade.

In saucepan, heat oil to 375° F and carefully transfer to fondue pot. Do not fill pot more than half full.

Spear steak and fondue 2 minutes, or until cooked to desired doneness.

2 Tbsp soy sauce
2 Tbsp water
2 green onions, minced
2 cloves garlic, minced
1 tsp sugar
1 tsp ground ginger
freshly ground black pepper to taste
1 Tbsp sesame seeds, toasted and crushed
1 lb flank steak, thinly sliced into 1 inch strips
    (easiest when partially frozen)
3-4 cups oil, for fondue

Serve with

Teriyaki Sauce (page 55), Thai Peanut Sauce (page 59), Wasabi Mayonnaise (page 63)

Fresh-cooked rice and steamed broccoli

Chinese Salad (page 66)

Serves 4

skewered beef in red wine

Combine first 10 ingredients in a large stockpot, making sure meat bones and vegetables are well-covered with water. Bring to a boil and simmer for 1½ hours, skimming foam off the top from time to time. Taste and salt if necessary.

Strain through a cheesecloth-lined sieve and discard solids.

Put the red wine into a metal fondue pot and bring to a boil on stove. Boil until reduced by half, then add the juniper berries, peppercorns, and strained stock. Add salt if needed. Return to a boil, transfer to tabletop burner, and continue to simmer.

Arrange a platter of sliced beef on a bed of lettuce for the table. Ask guests to thread a slice of beef onto a wooden skewer and cook in the simmering stock for 1-2 minutes.

Serves 6

3 lbs beef bones
1 onion, coarsely chopped
2 cloves garlic, halved
2 carrots, coarsely chopped
2 celery stalks, sliced
¼ tsp whole cloves
1 bay leaf
2 tsp salt
½ cup chopped fresh parsley
4 quarts water

1 cup red wine
1 Tbsp juniper berries
1 tsp black peppercorns
salt to taste
2½ lb beef tenderloin, finely sliced (easiest when partially frozen)
6 leaves Romaine lettuce

Serve with

Crusty baguette slices, whole mushrooms, and bermuda onion wedges threaded on wooden skewers for fonduing

Apple Horseradish Sauce (page 62), Remoulade Sauce (page 60), and Spiced Mustard (page59)

Greek Salad (page 65)

roast beef fondue

Cut partially frozen beef into long thin strips. Put in ziplock bag.

In a bowl, mix oil with soy sauce, honey, lemon peel, dried herbs, cognac, and salt, pepper, and cayenne to taste. Add to beef in bag, and marinade, turning occasionally, for two hours.

Heat beef broth to boiling and carefully pour into fondue pot. Transfer broth to tabletop burner and keep it simmering.

Remove beef from marinade and pat slices dry with paper towels. Put on a platter over a bed of Boston lettuce and place on the table. Roll up or thread a slice of beef onto skewer. Cook in simmering stock 2-3 minutes.

1½ pounds boneless beef loin, cut into thin strips
    (easiest when partially frozen)
¼ cup vegetable oil
2 Tbsp soy sauce
1 Tbsp honey
1 tsp grated lemon rind
1 Tbsp dried herbes de Provence
1 tsp cognac (optional)
dash salt, pepper, and cayenne pepper
4 quarts beef broth
1 head Boston lettuce

Serve with

Remoulade Sauce (page 60), Sweet & Sour Sauce (page 58), Danish Blue Cheese Sauce (page 56), and Aïoli Sauce (page 57)

Small red boiled or sautéed dill potatoes

Mixed Green Salad (page 67)

Serves 4

seafood cioppino fondue

In a very large kettle, heat the oil over medium heat. Add the carrot, onion, pepper, and garlic, and cook, stirring occasionally, for 10 minutes.

Add the mushrooms, tomato (and any accumulated juices), tomato paste, wine, bouillon, lemon slices, ½ cup of the parsley, oregano, and salt and pepper to taste.

Bring to a boil, reduce the heat, cover, and simmer for 20 minutes. Return to a boil, transfer the pot to its tabletop burner and keep simmering.

Spear the fish onto fondue forks and cook in the simmering broth 2-3 minutes. The shellfish and shrimp will cook first. Check after 1 minute to see if they are opened (and done). Dip in sauces.

When about ½ of the fish remains, add it to the fondue pot. Simmer slowly for 20 minutes.

Serve the cioppino in large bowls as soup; sprinkle with the remaining parsley.

Serves 6

½ teaspoon olive oil
½ lb carrots, peeled and coarsely chopped
1½ cups onion, coarsely chopped
1½ cups green bell pepper, coarsely chopped
1½ Tbsp garlic, finely chopped
¾ lb mushrooms, sliced
4 cups plum tomatoes, peeled and chopped
    or 1 (28 oz) can plum tomatoes, chopped
½ can (3 oz) tomato paste
1 cup dry red wine
1½ cups beef broth
½ lemon, thinly sliced (about ½ cup)
¾ cup Italian parsley, finely chopped
2 tsp dried oregano
Salt and freshly ground black pepper

½ lb swordfish, cut into 1 inch chunks
2 lbs lobster meat, cut into pieces
12 hard-shell clams, scrubbed
½ lb mussels, scrubbed and debearded
¾ lb halibut cut into 1 inch pieces
½ lb large shrimp, shelled and deveined

Serve with

Warm crusty-herb bread, Remoulade Sauce (page 60), Curried Cream Sauce (page 63)

Mixed Green Salad (page 67)

SEAFOOD
FONDUES

tuna steaks with kalamata sauce

To make Kalamata sauce, combine the olives, capers, mustard, anchovy paste, lemon juice, cognac, garlic, and red pepper flakes in a blender and puree. Place in a small bowl and stir in the mayonnaise. Cover and let stand for 1 hour at room temperature. Makes about 1 cup.

Fill metal fondue pot with oil, no more than half-full, and heat on stove until temperature reaches 375° F. Carefully transfer pot to a fondue burner with flame.

Cube tuna steaks and fondue 1-2 minutes in oil. Serve with the Kalamata sauce, along with additional sauces, rice, and salad.

Kalamata Sauce

¾ cup pitted Kalamata olives
2 Tbsp capers
1 Tbsp Dijon mustard
1 tsp anchovy paste
1 tsp fresh lemon juice
1 tsp cognac or brandy
2 garlic cloves, pressed
¼ tsp crushed hot red pepper flakes
½ cup mayonnaise

3-4 cups peanut or vegetable oil
2 lb (½ inch thick) tuna steaks, cut into ¾ inch cubes

Serve with

Kalamata Sauce, Remoulade Sauce (page 60), Wasabi Mayonnaise (page 63), and Aïoli Sauce (page 57)

Saffron rice

Cucumber Salad (page 69)

Serves 4

lemon coriander halibut

In a bowl combine first 7 marinade ingredients. Pour into a ziplock bag, add halibut, and toss to coat. Refrigerate for at least one hour.

Meanwhile, peel potato and put peelings in a medium saucepan. (Reserve potato for another use.) Add all ingredients and cover well with water. Bring to a boil, reduce heat and simmer, covered, for 1 hour. Strain liquid through a sieve, discarding solids.

Transfer vegetable broth to fondue pot and keep simmering.

Remove halibut from marinade and spear with fondue fork. Fondue for 2-4 minutes or until cooked through.

Serve with

Curried Cream Sauce (page 63), Wasabi Mayonnaise (page 63), and Teriyaki Sauce (page 55)

Grilled new potatoes with rosemary in foil

Orange-Blueberry Salad (page 71)

Serves 4

Marinade

¼ cup lemon juice
3 cloves garlic
2 Tbsp olive oil
2 tsp ground coriander
1 tsp finely grated lemon zest
½ tsp dried rosemary
¼ tsp dried thyme
1 lb halibut steaks, cubed

Broth

1 large potato (peeling only)
½ teaspoon olive oil
¼ large onion, chopped
2 carrots, peeled and chopped
2 stalks celery (with leaves) chopped
¼ zucchini (with skin) chopped
¼ cup diced sweet potato
2 cloves garlic, halved
½ cup chopped fresh parsley, leaves and stems
½ tsp dried thyme
1 tsp salt
3 peppercorns
5½ cups water

coconut shrimp fondue

Combine coconut milk and lime juice in a bowl.

In a second bowl, combine bread crumbs with curry powder, salt, and pepper.

Dip shrimp one at a time in coconut milk, then coat in bread crumbs. Place breaded shrimp on a platter and refrigerate for at least 15 minutes.

In a third bowl, beat egg. Place coconut and cayenne pepper on a plate. Dip shrimp in beaten egg, then roll in coconut until thoroughly coated.

In a saucepan heat oil to 375° F and transfer to fondue pot (or heat oil in an electric fondue pot). Do not fill pot more than half full.

Spear shrimp on fondue fork and fondue for 1 to 2 minutes or until golden brown.

⅓ cup unsweetened coconut milk
3 Tbsp fresh lime juice
¾ cup dry bread crumbs
1½ tsp curry powder
salt and freshly ground pepper to taste
1½ lbs jumbo shrimp
2 eggs, beaten
¾ cup unsweetened coconut, finely minced
⅓ tsp cayenne pepper
3-4 cups oil for fondue

Serve with

Wedges of kiwi fruit, Curried Cream Sauce (page 63), Mango Salsa (page 53), and Teriyaki Sauce (page 55)

Fresh-cooked basmati rice

Chinese Salad (page 66)

Serves 6

bagna cauda

Put anchovy fillets in coffee mug and cut up with scissors until finely minced.

Gently heat the oil, garlic, and anchovies in a small saucepan. Stir in the butter and cook over low heat for 2-3 minutes, making sure the garlic doesn't brown. Put in blender and puree to make an emulsion.

Transfer to a bowl and place over a candle burner to keep mixture warm.

Arrange vegetables and bread on platter. Dip into hot sauce.

10 anchovy fillets (about 2-3 oz), finely minced
¾ cup extra virgin olive oil
5 garlic cloves
4 Tbsp butter

Serve with

A variety of cut vegetables such as peppers, carrots, cauliflowers, broccoli, artichoke hearts, sugar snap peas, fennel, grape tomatoes

Breadsticks or cubed sourdough bread

Orange and Blueberry Salad (page 71)

Serves 4 to 6

VEGETABLE
FONDUES

tempura vegetable fondue

Rinse and cut vegetables into thin strips.

Prepare batter in a bowl as follows: Separate egg. Then, using a whisk, beat the yolk with the water, flour, and 1 teaspoon of the sesame oil until smooth. Whisk the egg white until stiff, then stir into the batter, cover, and leave for 30 minutes.

Fill fondue pot no more than half full with oil. Heat the oil and the remaining 2 teaspoons sesame oil to 375° F and carefully place over the lit burner.

Spear the vegetables onto the fondue forks and dip into the prepared batter, then into the hot oil. Fondue for two minutes or until golden.

2 lbs assorted fresh vegetables, such as eggplant, baby corn, mushrooms, asparagus, water chestnuts, assorted bell peppers, peapods, and broccoli florets

1 medium egg, separated
⅔ cup ice-cold water
1 cup flour
3 tsp sesame oil
3-4 cups oil, for frying

Serve with

Teriyaki Sauce (page 55), Sweet & Sour Sauce (page 58), and Wasabi Mayonnaise (page 63)

Fresh-cooked sushi rice

Asian Sesame Salad (page 73)

Serves 6

ginger tofu fondue

To make marinade, mix together first 4 ingredients in a small bowl. Pour into a ziplock bag and add tofu, mixing well. Refrigerate one hour or more.

Meanwhile, peel potato and put peelings in a medium saucepan. Add all ingredients and cover with water. Bring to a boil, reduce heat and simmer, covered, for 1 hour. Strain liquid through a sieve, discarding solids. Transfer vegetable broth to fondue pot and keep simmering.

With a slotted spoon, transfer tofu from bag to a platter. Pour remaining marinade into a small bowl to use as a dipping sauce. Add assorted vegetables to tofu platter.

Spear tofu and vegetables with fondue fork and fondue for three minutes. Dip in marinade and other dipping sauces.

Serve with

Sweet & Sour Sauce (page 58), Teriyaki Sauce (page 55), and Thai Peanut Sauce (page 59)

Basmati rice and Apple-Cranberry Salad (page 72)

Marinade

¼ cup soy sauce

3 tablespoons ginger root, minced

2 tablespoons sugar

2 tablespoons sesame oil

12 ounces extra-firm tofu, squeezed dry with paper towels to extract water, and then cubed

1½ lbs assorted vegetables

Broth

1 large potato (peeling only)

½ teaspoon olive oil

¼ large onion, chopped

2 carrots, peeled and chopped

2 stalks celery (with leaves) chopped

¼ zucchini (with skin) chopped

¼ cup diced sweet potato

2 cloves garlic, halved

½ cup chopped fresh parsley, leaves and stems

½ tsp dried thyme

1 tsp salt

3 peppercorns

5½ cups water

Serves 4

asparagus fondue

Sauté the garlic and asparagus in the apple juice for 5 minutes, until softened. Add the sherry and stir gently until blended. When hot, pour into the fondue pot and place over the lit burner.

In a small bowl, toss cheese in the cornstarch. Then slowly add handfuls of the cheese to pot and stir until cheese has melted. Season with the hot sauce and black pepper. Cook until thick and creamy.

3 cloves garlic, crushed
8 fresh asparagus spears, chopped
1¼ cups apple juice
2 Tbsp sherry
3 cups Gruyère cheese, grated
2 Tbsp cornstarch
hot sauce, to taste
freshly ground black pepper

Serve with

Fresh steamed asparagus spears, red pepper slivers, carrot sticks, and mushrooms for dipping

Sautéed red potatoes with caramelized onions

Greek Salad (page 65)

Serves 4

SAUCES

fruit or vegetable salsa

In a medium bowl, combine all the ingredients. Allow to stand for 30 minutes before serving to blend the flavors.

Most salsas are best eaten the day they are made, but they will keep for several days, covered and refrigerated. Experiment beyond the classic tomato and cilantro salsa to mango and tomatillo, or cherries with orange zest and basil. One of my favorites is papaya and black bean.

2 cups ripe fruit or vegetables, singly or in combination, such as peeled, diced tomatoes, mangoes, papayas, pineapple, halved and pitted cherries, cooked drained black beans, diced roasted red peppers, or tomatillos

3 serrano or jalapeño chiles, minced

¼ cup chopped fresh herbs, singly or in combination, such as cilantro, basil, flat-leaf parsley, or chives

1 teaspoon honey

2 tablespoons fresh lime juice (or orange juice with fruits)

½ teaspoon salt

Makes 2 cups

el diablo sauce

Place all ingredients in blender and puree for a few seconds. Chill completely.

1 cup (8 oz) tomato puree
2 small hot green chili peppers, minced
1½ tsp olive oil
1½ tsp red wine vinegar
¼ tsp oregano
¼ tsp cumin powder
Pinch each garlic salt and ground cloves

Makes 1 cup

chervil sauce

Blend the cheese with lemon juice, salt and pepper. Beat in the olive oil slowly, as if making mayonnaise. Continue beating until fluffy. Mix in chervil. Taste for seasoning, cover and refrigerate.

Chervil is one of the *fines herbes* and more delicate than parsley.

1 (6 oz) pkg Gervais or Philadelphia cream cheese
1 tsp lemon juice
Dash salt (if cream cheese is used)
Dash white pepper
6 Tbsp olive or vegetable oil
1 Tbsp dried or fresh chervil

Makes 1 cup

green goddess sauce

Mix all ingredients and chill 24 hours.

1 very ripe avocado
1 (2 oz) can flat anchovies, minced
1 cup mayonnaise
½ cup sour cream
3 Tbsp minced green onions
¼ cup minced parsley
1 Tbsp lemon juice
1 Tbsp white or tarragon vinegar
1 small clove garlic, pressed
Salt and pepper to taste

Makes 2 cups

teriyaki sauce

Bring all ingredients to a boil in saucepan.
Let simmer until reduced to one cup.

1 cup dry sherry or dry Madeira
½ cup soy sauce
¼ tsp grated ginger or pinch powdered ginger
1 Tbsp sugar

Makes 1 cup

guacamole del diablo sauce

Place ingredients in bowl and blend until thoroughly combined. Stir in tomato.

2 ripe avocados, mashed
1 small jalapeño pepper, minced
1½ Tbsp onion, minced
1 clove garlic, minced
2 Tbsp lime juice
1 ripe tomato, diced

Makes 1 cup

danish blue cheese sauce

Blend cheese and sour cream well. Mix in thyme, bruising the leaves well before adding. Add lemon juice to taste.

½ cup crumbled Danish blue cheese
½ cup sour cream
1 tsp freshly chopped thyme or ½ tsp dried thyme
Few drops lemon juice

Makes 1 cup

aïoli sauce

Place garlic in a mortar or small deep-sided bowl. With a pestle or wooden spoon, begin mashing it, adding salt a pinch at a time until garlic is reduced to a paste. Drop the egg yolk into garlic and mix well. When thoroughly blended and thick, begin adding the oil, drop by drop, whisking fast with a wire whisk. When half the oil has been added in this manner, you can increase the flow to a thin stream—but be careful that all oil is blending in. When as thick as mayonnaise, add lemon juice. Chill slightly.

2 cloves garlic, minced
Salt
1 egg yolk (at room temperature)
⅔ cup olive oil
Juice of ½ lemon (1 Tbsp)

Makes ¾ cup

sweet and sour sauce

Heat the oil in a pan and gently sauté the pepper and scallions for 2 minutes. Add pineapple (reserving ⅓ of the juice) and sauté one minute.

Add the chicken broth, soy sauce, vinegar, ginger, and honey, bring to a boil, and simmer for 4 minutes.

Blend the cornstarch with the reserved pineapple juice, stir into the sauce, and cook, stirring until the sauce thickens.

1 Tbsp oil
1 red bell pepper, seeded and chopped
6 scallions, roughly chopped (white part left whole)
6 slices canned pineapple, diced (reserve ⅓ of the juice)
⅔ cup chicken broth
1 Tbsp soy sauce
1 Tbsp red wine vinegar
2 Tbsp chopped preserved ginger
2 tsp honey
2 Tbsp cornstarch
⅓ cup reserved pineapple juice

Makes 2 cups

thai peanut sauce

Combine all ingregients in a small bowl and mix well. Cover and refrigerate.

¼ cup honey

2 Tbsp rice vinegar

3 Tbsp peanut butter

2 Tbsp soy sauce

3 Tbsp sesame oil

3 cloves garlic, minced

1 Tbsp minced ginger root

½ tsp red pepper flakes

Makes ¾ cup

spiced mustard sauce

Combine all ingredients and chill for a few hours.

1 cup sour cream

2 Tbsp Dijon mustard

1 Tbsp soy sauce

1 Tbsp Worcestershire sauce

1 tsp grated onion

1 clove garlic, crushed

Salt and pepper to taste

Makes 1½ cups

remoulade sauce

Mix all ingredients well. Chill thoroughly.
Garnish with chopped chives.

1 cup mayonnaise
1 Tbsp chopped pickled gherkins
1 Tbsp chopped parsley
1 Tbsp drained, chopped capers
1 tsp prepared hot mustard
1 small clove garlic, minced
hot pepper sauce to taste
1 Tbsp chopped chives

Makes 1¾ cups

apple horseradish dip

In a bowl combine apple, horseradish, mayonnaise, sour cream, lemon juice, and sugar; mix well. Cover and refrigerate overnight to allow flavors to blend. Bring to room temperature before serving.

1 tart apple, peeled and grated
¼ cup prepared horseradish
¼ cup mayonnaise
¼ cup sour cream
1 Tbsp fresh lemon juice
1 tsp brown sugar

Makes 1½ cup

kalamata sauce

Combine the olives, capers, mustard, anchovy paste, lemon juice, cognac, garlic, and red pepper flakes in a blender and puree. Place in a small bowl and stir in the mayonnaise. Let stand one hour at room temperature to allow the flavors to blend.

½ cup pitted Kalamata olives
2 Tbsp capers
1 Tbsp Dijon mustard
1 tsp anchovy paste
1 teaspoon fresh lemon juice
1 tsp cognac or brandy
2 garlic cloves, pressed
¼ teaspoon crushed hot red pepper flakes
½ cup mayonnaise

Makes 1 cup

wasabi mayonnaise

Combine mayonnaise and wasabi in a small bowl and mix well. Cover and refrigerate at least one hour to allow flavors to blend. Bring to room temperature before serving.

¾ cup mayonnaise
2 Tbsp wasabi powder

Makes ¾ cup

curried cream sauce

Combine all ingredients. Taste for seasoning. Add more curry powder or lemon juice if desired.

½ cup mayonnaise
2 Tbsp curry powder
½ cup sour cream
1 tsp lemon juice

Makes 1 cup

SALADS

greek salad

Spread lettuce on large platter with onion slices on top.

Arrange ingredients in overlapping concentric circles starting at the outside edge of the platter and moving toward the center: tomatoes, bell peppers, cucumber, eggs, cheese, olives, and pepperonici.

Sprinkle oregano over all.

Dressing

In medium bowl, combine and beat ingredients with wire whisk, adding oil very gradually. Beat to triple thickness. Pour dressing over the salad just before serving.

1 head romaine lettuce, washed, spun dry, and torn
¼ purple onion, thinly sliced
5 roma tomatoes, thinly sliced
1 yellow bell pepper, seeded and thinly sliced
1 hothouse English cucumber, peeled and thinly sliced
4 hard-cooked eggs, thinly sliced
½ lb feta cheese, cubed or crumbled
8 Kalamata olives
4 pepperonici salad peppers
1 Tbsp Greek oregano

Dressing

1 clove garlic, minced
⅓ cup red wine vinegar
1 tsp lemon juice
¼ tsp salt
8 grinds fresh pepper (¼ tsp)
2 tsp Greek oregano
1 tsp honey
½ cup extra virgin olive oil

Makes 1 cup

Serves 6

chinese salad

Combine first six dressing ingredients in blender and puree 30 seconds. Add oil slowly.

Place the bok choy in a large serving bowl with the green onions. Add the cucumbers, celery, bell pepper, and bean sprouts.

Just before serving, toss the salad with the dressing. Sprinkle with the chopped cilantro and peanuts.

2 cups bok choy, rinsed and finely shredded

8 green onions, trimmed and chopped

½ small European cucumber, peeled, sliced, and cut into half-moon shapes

4 celery stalks, trimmed and chopped

1 red bell pepper, seeded and diced

2 cups bean sprouts

3 Tbsp fresh cilantro, chopped

4 Tbsp unsalted roasted peanuts, chopped

Ginger Dressing

¼ cup soy sauce

¼ cup rice vinegar

2 green onions, chopped

2 Tbsp fresh ginger root, peeled and chopped

2 tsp honey

¼ tsp hot sauce

¼ tsp sesame oil

Makes ¾ cup

Serves 6

mixed green salad

Place the artichoke hearts in a bowl. Rinse the tomatoes, slice and add to the bowl.

Wipe the mushrooms and add to the bowl, along with the olives.

Put all the ingredients for the vinaigrette in a bowl except the oil. Add oil very slowly and beat to a triple thickness.

Line the salad bowl with the salad leaves, then place the salad ingredients in the center. Dress salad with the vinaigrette at the last minute.

2 cups bottled artichoke hearts, drained
1 cup cherry or roma tomatoes, sliced
1 cup mushrooms, sliced
¼ cup pitted Kalamata olives
6 cups hearts of romaine leaves, rinsed and spun dry

World's Best Vinaigrette

4 cloves garlic, pressed
2 anchovies, minced
1 tsp salt
½ tsp freshly ground pepper
¼ cup balsamic vinegar
2 tsp Dijon mustard
2 tsp honey
¼ cup olive oil
¼ cup vegetable oil

Makes ¾ cup

Serves 4

mushroom salad

Put the garlic, green onions, and vinegar into a blender and puree. Add the sugar and salt. Add oil gradually in a steady stream. When thick, add the lemon juice and pepper. Cover and refrigerate.

Cut mushrooms into very thin slices. Arrange the lettuce on six salad plates. Arrange the mushrooms, artichokes, tomatoes, walnuts, and blue cheese on top of the lettuce. Drizzle each salad with dressing and serve immediately.

6 large mushrooms, wiped clean and sliced thin
8 cups Boston and red leaf lettuce, torn
1 (16 oz) can artichoke hearts, cut in half
About 24 cherry tomatoes, cut in half
⅓ cup walnuts, toasted
4 ounces blue cheese, crumbled

Dressing

2 cloves garlic, pressed
4 green onions including stems, sliced
¼ cup cider vinegar
2 Tbsp sugar
½ tsp salt
1¼ cups vegetable oil
1 Tbsp fresh lemon juice
Freshly ground black pepper, to taste

Makes 1¾ cups

Serves 6

cucumbers with dill

Cut each scored cucumber into ¼-inch-thick diagonal slices. Place into a large bowl. In a small saucepan, heat the vinegar, sugar, and salt over low heat, stirring until sugar dissolves. Cool; pour over cucumbers. Stir in the dill. Cover; chill for 2 hours or more, stirring occasionally. Place on a serving platter, season with pepper, and garnish with dill sprigs.

2 unpeeled European cucumbers, scored
    lengthwise with the tines of a fork
⅔ cup white wine vinegar
2 heaping Tbsp sugar
½ tsp salt
4 Tbsp minced fresh dill
freshly ground black pepper
fresh dill sprigs, for garnish

Serves 6

orange and blueberry salad

Rinse and drain the blueberries.

In a large bowl, whisk together the sugar, vinegar, onion, and salt. Gently mix in the blueberries. Cover and refrigerate for 30 minutes or up to 2 days.

Spread the frisée greens evenly over a large platter.

Peel the oranges, removing as much of the white membrane as possible. Cut into thin slices. Place in a wide circle on the bed of greens, slightly overlapping.

With a slotted spoon, scoop the blueberries inside the circle of orange slices. Spoon the blueberry marinade over the salad; drizzle with the olive oil. Season with pepper. Scatter the pecans over the oranges. Serve at once.

1 pint fresh blueberries
¼ cup packed light brown sugar
2 Tbsp balsamic vinegar
2 Tbsp finely minced red onion
pinch of salt
8 cups frisée, watercress, mesclun, arugula or
    "Spring Mix" rinsed and spun dry
5 navel oranges, peeled and sliced
4 Tbsp extra virgin olive oil
coarsely ground black pepper, to taste
⅓ cup toasted pecans, chopped

Serves 6

apple-cranberry salad

In blender or medium bowl, whisk together vinegar, sugar, salt, and pepper. Whisk oil in drop by drop. Refrigerate, covered.

Divide salad greens among 6 salad plates; top with tomatoes, apples, cranberries, cheese, and pecans. Drizzle vinaigrette over salads; serve immediately.

8 cups mixed greens, rinsed and spun dry
24 grape tomatoes, cut in half
2 tart apples, cored, diced, and held in a 50% lemon juice and water solution
¾ cup dried cranberries
8 ounces shredded cheddar cheese
⅓ cup pecans, toasted and chopped

Raspberry Vinaigrette

¼ cup raspberry vinegar
4 Tbsp sugar
2 tsp Dijon mustard
¼ tsp salt
⅛ tsp ground pepper
½ cup olive oil

Makes ¾ cups

Serves 6

In a medium bowl, whisk sugar, mustard, salt, Worcestershire sauce, and vinegar. Whisk in oil very slowly. Toast sesame seeds in butter in a skillet. Add sesame seeds to dressing. Cover and refrigerate.

Divide salad greens among 6 salad plates; top with orange slices, carrots, cabbage, noodles, and almonds. Splash dressing over salads; serve immediately.

10 cups salad greens, rinsed and dried
1 (11 oz) can Mandarin orange slices, drained
½ cup shredded carrots
½ cup shredded red cabbage
½ cup crunchy Asian chow mein noodles
½ cup sliced almonds, toasted

Sesame Seed Dressing

⅓ cup sugar
¼ tsp dry mustard
½ tsp salt
½ tsp Worcestershire sauce
½ cup cider vinegar
1 cup vegetable oil
⅓ cup sesame seeds, toasted
1 tsp butter

Makes 1¾ cups

Serves 6

classic chocolate fondue

Warm cream first, then add chocolate, chopped into small pieces. Stir in the kirsch.

This classic fondue may be varied by substituting ¼ teaspoon ground cloves and ¼ teaspoon cinnamon for the liqueur.

½ cup cream
3 (3 oz) bars of quality bittersweet chocolate, such as Toblerone or Lindt, chopped
2 Tbsp kirsch, cognac, or Cointreau

Serve with

Strawberries, Kiwi, bananas, starfruit, mango, pineapple, cherries for dipping on wooden skewers

Serves 4

DESSERT
FONDUES

white chocolate fondue

Warm cream first; then add zest of 1 lemon, and white chocolate, chopped into small pieces. Melt over low flame, then add liqueur.

There is a white chocolate candy bar containing cocoa butter and crushed almonds which can be used in this recipe.

½ cup cream
zest of 1 lemon
3 (3 oz) bars quality white chocolate, chopped
2 Tbsp Amaretto liqueur

Serve with

Blueberries, bing cherries, and amaretti cookies for dipping

Serves 4

chocolate mint fondue

Warm cream first. Then add chocolate, chopped into small pieces, over low flame. Add the liqueur, one tablespoon at a time, to taste. Add more cream if desired.

⅓ cup cream
12 oz Andes or After Eight mints
2 Tbsp crème de menthe

Serve with

Strawberries, pineapple chunks, bananas, ladyfinger cookies, and raspberry scones for dipping

Serves 4

maple rum chocolate delight

Melt ice cream in the fondue pot with the maple syrup, stirring well. Mix rum with cornstarch. When ice cream has melted, add the rum mixture and stir well. Keep hot over a very low flame.

1 pint very rich chocolate ice cream
½ cup pure maple syrup
2 Tbsp rum or Godiva liqueur
2 tsp cornstarch

Serve with

Cantalope, mango wedges, and shortbread cookies for dipping

Serves 4

orange chocolate

Warm cream. Then add chopped chocolate over low flame. Add liqueur.

½ cup cream
3 (3 oz) orange-flavored Lindt chocolate bars, chopped
2 Tbsp Grand Marnier or Cointreau

Serve with

Orange sections, starfruit slices, grapes, and ginger cookies for dipping

Serves 4

fudge with port

Warm cream first, then stir in the chocolate, chopped into small pieces. Melt over low flame. When hot and thinned, stir in the port. Heat thoroughly.

The chocolate and cream in this recipe can be replaced with 1 cup milk chocolate fudge topping.

½ cup cream
3 (3 oz) bars of quality semi-swet chocolate, such as Toblerone or Lindt, chopped
¼ cup port

Serve with

Apple wedges, pears, apricots, and banana-bread cubes for dipping

Serves 4

raspberry chocolate

Warm cream first, then add chocolate chopped into small pieces. Melt over low flame, then add liqueur.

½ cup cream
3 (3 oz) bars of quality chocolate, chopped
2 Tbsp raspberry liqueur

Serve with

Peach slices, pears, tangerine sections, biscotti, and chocolate chip cookies for dipping

Serves 4

In the top of a double boiler, over non-boiling hot water, combine sugar, coffee, chocolates, and cream, stirring constantly until melted and smooth. Remove from heat. Stir in Tia Maria and vanilla. Transfer immediately to dessert fondue pot over candle flame. Do not allow chocolate to boil.

1½ cups powdered sugar

⅓ cup strong coffee or espresso

3 ounces semi-sweet chocolate, chopped

3 ounces unsweetened chocolate, chopped

½ cup whipping cream

1 Tbsp Tia Maria

1 tsp vanilla extract

Serve with

Sponge cake cubes, shortbread cookies, dried apricots, grapes, and strawberries for dipping

Serves 4

pineapple fondue

In the top of a double boiler over boiling water, combine pineapple juice, reserved pineapple syrup, sugar, and cornstarch; cook, stirring constantly, for 3 to 5 minutes or until thickened.

Remove from heat. Stir in lemon juice, cinnamon, and crushed pineapple.

Stir in Cointreau. Transfer immediately to tabletop dessert fondue pot over candle flame.

1 cup pineapple juice
¾ cup crushed pineapple, drained, ¼ cup syrup reserved
3 Tbsp sugar
2 Tbsp cornstarch
1 Tbsp lemon juice
½ tsp ground cinnamon
4 tsp Cointreau

Serve with

Amaretti cookies, banana-bread cubes, dried apricots, mango, banana, and kiwi slices for dipping

Serves 4

cherry supreme fondue

In a small bowl, stir together cornstarch and water to dissolve.

Warm cherry syrup in a saucepan over medium heat. Whisk in dissolved cornstarch and sugar; stir over low heat for 5 minutes or until thickened.

Stir in halved cherries; simmer, uncovered, for 20 minutes. Add kirsch and stir well. If sauce is too thick, add more kirsch.

Transfer immediately to dessert fondue pot over tabletop candle flame.

2 Tbsp cornstarch
2 Tbsp water
1 (14 oz) can sour cherries, pitted and halved, syrup drained and reserved
3 Tbsp sugar
4 tsp lemon juice
2 Tbsp kirsch

Serve with

Chocolate cookies, cubed pound cake, peach wedges, or cubed kiwi for dipping; or serve over vanilla ice cream

Serves 4

strawberry, blackberry, or raspberry cream fondue

Boil the water and sugar together for five minutes. Add the berries and cook until soft. Stir in the lemon juice and puree the fruit in a blender. Then puree into a strainer to remove seeds, with the saucepan below the strainer.

Return the saucepan to the stove and heat gently until warm. Stir in the cream. Mix brandy or port with cornstarch and stir in. Heat until thickened.

¾ cup water
¼ cup sugar
2 cups blackberries, unsweetened strawberries, or raspberries
1 Tbsp lemon juice
2 Tbsp blackberry brandy or port
½ cup heavy cream
1 Tbsp cornstarch

Serve with

cubed pound cake, apple wedges, starfruit, and chocolate chip cookies for dipping

Serves 6

lemon mascarpone fondue

Place the mascarpone, sugar, and amaretto into a small heatproof ceramic bowl set over a saucepan of simmering water. Heat, stirring, until smooth. Stir in the lemon juice. Transfer the mixture to its tabletop burner to keep warm.

10 ounces mascarpone cheese
⅓ cup powdered sugar
2 Tbsp Amaretto liqueur
1 tsp fresh lemon juice

Serve with

Sliced nectarines, green grapes, peaches, toasted whole almonds, chocolate biscuits, and almond cookies for dipping

Serves 6

Combine sugar and cornstarch in a saucepan over medium heat. Slowly pour in boiling water, stirring constantly, until mixture comes to a boil. Reduce heat and simmer for 5 minutes or until thickened. Remove from heat and stir in melted butter and vanilla.

Transfer immediately to a dessert fondue pot over tabletop candle flame.

½ cup granulated sugar
2 Tbsp plus 1 tsp cornstarch
1¼ cups boiling water
3 Tbsp butter, melted
2 tsp vanilla extract, "white" if available

Serve with

Chocolate-covered coffee beans, peach slices, blueberries, dried cranberries, kiwi slices, and cubed dense chocolate cake for dipping

Serves 4

NOTES:

NOTES:

NOTES:

INDEX

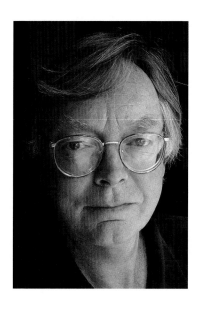

Jerry Stebbins, in the course of a career spanning almost thirty years, has worked for magazines such as *National Geographic, Time, Fortune,* and *Discover.* His discerning eye as a nature and landscape photographer is also on display in three books, *Boundary Waters, Mississippi River,* and *Over Minnesota.* In recent years he has worked almost exclusively as a commercial advertising photographer out of his St. Paul studio.

Susan Lukens has spent more than twenty years developing recipes and arranging food for the camera. Her clients range from giant corporations to fledgling restaurants. She brings precision and grace to whatever she does, be it television commercials or Japanese flower arranging, but she never feels more at home than when developing innovative recipes to enjoy with friends and family.